BIRDS
OF AUSTRALIA

Steve Parish

THE SIGNATURE COLLECTION

Above: The Crimson Rosella is seen in the coastal forests of eastern Australia.

Previous page: A Rainbow Lorikeet, one of a group of nectar-eating parrots.

The Laughing Kookaburra is a giant kingfisher, whose chuckling territorial call is heard at dawn and dusk across Australia's bushland. It has adapted well to life in towns and cities.

CONTENTS

7	INTRODUCTION
8	**BIRDS OF THE BUSHLANDS**
9	SWEET-SINGING BUSH BIRDS
11	SWIFT-FLYING FLOWER-SEEKERS
15	RAINBOWS OF THE FORESTS
16	COCKATOO PORTRAITS
19	FASCINATING FINCHES
21	MASTER BUILDERS – THE BOWERBIRDS
22	SINGERS AND CALLERS
25	HUNTERS OF THE NIGHT
26	FROGMOUTHS: KOOKABURRAS OF THE NIGHT
28	A TASTE OF HONEY
30	**BIRDS OF THE ARIDLANDS**
31	LIVING IN A DRY CONTINENT
33	CLOWNS IN THE DESERT
37	BIRDS OF PREY
39	EMU AND AUSTRALIAN BUSTARD
42	**BIRDS OF THE RAINFORESTS**
43	SINGING IN THE GREEN FORESTS
45	CLOAKS OF MANY COLOURS
47	RAINFOREST PIGEONS
49	REGENTS RULE, OKAY?
50	HELMETED HERO OF THE RAINFOREST
53	IN THE FOLIAGE AND ON THE FOREST FLOOR
57	RULERS IN THEIR OWN FOREST KINGDOM
58	**BIRDS OF THE WETLANDS**
59	WADERS, DIVERS AND AQUABATS
60	PREDATORS OF COASTS AND ESTUARIES
63	LORD OF THE WATERS
65	WITH A SILVER SPOON
68	DAGGER-BILLED GEMS
70	THERE'S SAFETY IN NUMBERS
73	WATERBIRDS OF NIGHT AND DAY
74	BEAUTIES OF THE BILLABONGS
79	IT TAKES THREE TO RAISE BABIES
80	**BIRDS OF THE COASTS**
81	A NEVER-ENDING COASTLINE OF BIRDS
84	BIRD OF THE TROPIC SEAS
87	SEAFRONT SCAVENGERS
91	DIVING FOR DINNER
93	BIRDS ON A CORAL CAY
94	MAP OF AUSTRALIAN HABITATS
95	WHY WATCH BIRDS?
96	INDEX

INTRODUCTION

The first feathered creatures to catch my attention were seabirds. As a child, I discovered the world of the seashore and the shallows; the gulls hanging around the beach and the terns hovering past the breakers and plunge-diving for fish fascinated me. I wanted to be up there in the air with them, wandering on wings across the ocean and along the coast, free to catch the winds to adventure.

As time passed, I began to watch the birds in our backyard, in the bushland outside the city, and on rivers and swamps. I wondered why kookaburras laughed in chorus at sunrise, and why magpies flew patrol at sunset, dipping first one wing then the other to display their warning colours. I saw herons and egrets catching fish and frogs, bulges travelling down their long neck as they gulped their victims down.

In my teens, I joined the navy, and later entered the national parks and wildlife service as a photographer. I took pictures of every bird that came within reach of my 600 mm lens and learnt everything I could about their behaviour. My collection of bird images grew, and every image increased my interest in the original creature.

This book contains pictures of birds taken all over Australia in a variety of habitats. The birds themselves are simply superb – gorgeous parrots in varied moods, elegant waterbirds in billabongs and wetlands, seabirds in vigorous action on coral reef, beach and ocean, birds of prey, finches, robins, and many more.

Birds are living jewels, gifted with the miraculous power of flight. Australia and its neighbouring seas are home to over 760 species, including groups found nowhere else in the world. Within the covers of this book are some of my favourites.

Steve Parish

Opposite: A Black-necked Stork, or Jabiru, preens its plumage with its long beak.

BIRDS OF THE BUSHLANDS

SWEET-SINGING BUSH BIRDS

The birds of the bush are a varied group. Some species, such as the robins and fairy-wrens, were named by British settlers for their superficial resemblance to birds "back home". Others, such as the pardalotes, are unique to Australia.

Their bushland homes are tracts of tall trees, often eucalypts, alternating with slighter acacias, banksias and, near water, callistemons and casuarinas. Native grasses and flowering annuals cover the open spaces between the trees. Much bushland depends on seasonal rains — winter in southern Australia, summer in the north — and many of the plants can survive moderate bushfires. Some even depend on occasional fires to scorch their seeds into opening.

Many bushland birds have special links with the continent's flora. The honeyeaters, lorikeets, woodswallows and others eat flower nectar and insects that gather around the blossom. These birds transport pollen from one flower to the next and are important fertilising agents. Some of Australia's most notable songsters live in bushland, and it is impossible for those who camp there to be unmoved by the beauty of the dawn chorus.

Opposite: Green plumage and bright head patches camouflage this Purple-crowned Lorikeet.
Above: The breast of the male Scarlet Robin is far brighter than that of the female.

This Rainbow Lorikeet is excited or aggressive, and is signalling its emotional state by raising its head and nape feathers. Like many brilliantly plumaged birds, it nests in tree hollows.

SWIFT-FLYING FLOWER-SEEKERS

Flocks of lorikeets are common sights when nectar-bearing trees are in flower. These small parrots swoop across the sky like a shrieking mass of sharp-tipped boomerangs with stubby heads and long, pointed tails. After plundering blossoms of their sweetness with their long, mop-tipped tongues, the lorikeets sit preening, making sure every sticky drop is cleaned from the short, stiff feathers on their breasts and backs. A pair will perch together, preening themselves and then nibbling each other's head feathers.

Rainbow Lorikeets are common on the coastal lowlands of northern and eastern Australia and have been introduced to Perth, Western Australia. They will learn quickly where food is available and will readily come to feeding tables in suburban gardens. Sugar and bread are not ideal for them; the best offering is a special, commercial lorikeet mix.

Rainbow Lorikeets preen after delving into flowers for sweet, sticky nectar. When they fly, they show a bright crimson flash under each wing.

The Eastern Rosella was first recorded at Rose Hill near Sydney (now known as Parramatta).

The settlers called it the Rose Hill parrot, which became rosehiller, then rosella.

A Crimson Rosella eating acacia seeds. Like all parrots, it holds food in one foot, then twists the food-holding leg so that it eats from the back, or outside, of the foot.

RAINBOWS OF THE FORESTS

Rosellas are colourful, broad-tailed parrots that have cheek patches of blue, white or yellow. The Crimson Rosella that is shown here is one of the blue-cheeked group. It is very variable in colour – the drier the country it lives in, the paler the plumage. In the forests of New South Wales and Victoria, the adult is vivid crimson, and younger birds have greenish feathers on back and belly. Towards Adelaide, the crimson in the plumage shades to orange. In the western Murray–Darling basin, the crimson has been replaced by yellow, though the forehead is still red and the cheek patches blue.

Flocks of Crimson Rosellas wander widely along forest edges searching for seeds and fruit to eat. Younger birds roam more than adult, mated pairs.

The Crimson Rosella is a seed- and fruit-eater. It has blue cheek patches rather than the white ones of the Eastern Rosella.

COCKATOO PORTRAITS

The name cockatoo comes from "kakatua", a Malay word, and these large parrots are found only in the Australasian region. Cockatoos have broad tails and crests that are erected when the birds are excited. Their plumages are mostly white or black, with patches of red, pink or yellow. Some Australian species, such as the black-cockatoos, are not common; the Glossy Black-Cockatoo is growing rarer, as are the Gang-gang Cockatoo and the Long-billed Corella. The Sulphur-crested Cockatoo and Galah, on the other hand, seem to be extending their ranges as water and grain become more easily available.

Preening each other reinforces the lifelong pair-bond between these Yellow-tailed Black-Cockatoos. It also grooms places each bird could not reach itself.

The Sulphur-crested Cockatoo may live to more than 80 years of age. It is a bird that needs large spaces in which to roam and a flock of lively companions with which to socialise.

The Long-tailed Finch's bill ranges from yellow to red, depending on where it lives. They are found across the north of the continent from the Kimberley in Western Australia to western Queensland.

FASCINATING FINCHES

Finches are small, often colourful, seed-eating birds whose stout, conical beaks are adapted for crushing seed. They are often seen in flocks, sometimes in large numbers. Australia has 17 species of finch; most live in areas where there is good rainfall and thus plentiful grass growth. Aridland species must live near permanent water.

Finches build large globes of grass with spout-like entrances as nests. Courtship displays often consist of one partner, male or female, holding a piece of grass and displaying to the other with it. The chicks, which live in semi-darkness, show colourful, light patches at the backs of their mouths – these guide the parents to deposit food in the right place.

A Red-browed Finch displaying with a feather rather than grass. A display mixes movement, postures and songs, and is used to communicate with other birds, usually of the same species.

A male Great Bowerbird builds a substantial platform and avenue of sticks around which he sings and displays. Females visit the bower to mate, young males to learn how to build.

MASTER BUILDERS – THE BOWERBIRDS

Bowerbird males spend their youth learning to build "bowers" and their mature years constructing and maintaining them. A bower is an avenue or platform built of sticks, sometimes decorated with paint, lichens and flowers. The bower serves as a focus for collections of flowers, fruits, bones and other objects. Each species has its own type of bower and its own types of "treasures".

Bowerbird females patrol the bowers in their areas, watching each resident male display by singing and posturing, often while holding one of his treasures. The male with the best bower and display is chosen as a mate. When they have mated (often in the bower), the female flies away. She builds a stick nest, lays eggs in it, incubates them and cares for the chicks. The male, meanwhile, resumes his displays, often observed by other, younger males that rearrange both bower and treasures when the resident male leaves to find food.

A Great Bowerbird brings a new piece of sun-bleached bone to his bower. It will be arranged carefully with the bird's other treasures.

SINGERS AND CALLERS

All birds produce sounds by forcing air through membranes that stretch across their voice boxes. The tautness of each membrane is controlled by muscles: for a low note the membrane is relaxed while for a high note it is tightened.

The group of birds known as passerines, or songbirds, has many adjusting muscles and group members make some of the world's most beautiful sounds. About half of Australia's bird species, including the lyrebirds, butcherbirds, magpie, whipbird, fairy-wrens and honeyeaters, are songbirds. Many of them have ringing, melodious songs that announce ownership of a territory or attract a mate. Mimicry of other species and environmental sounds is sometimes part of a song. It is often used in soft, meditative "whisper songs".

A bird's call is a short, often repeated sound or group of sounds typical of the bird's species. It communicates location, warning or some other basic fact to other birds of the species. Most birds call, though not all sing.

In the breeding season, birds such as this fairy-wren sing to announce their nesting territory. After chicks leave the nest, family members locate each other by calling.

The Rainbow Bee-eater has a distinctive "prrrp-prrrp" call. It is a migratory bird, and flock members that call in flight are probably keeping in contact with each other.

The Barking Owl is one of the hawk-owls. Members of this group have light-coloured eyes surrounded by a feathery disc. They eat insects, birds and mammals.

HUNTERS OF THE NIGHT

Owls are seldom seen flying during the day. They are night hunters, and daytime birds harass them by making alarm calls and swooping at them. At night, however, the owl comes into its own. Members of the dark-eyed barn owl group can hunt in total darkness, flying noiselessly on soft-edged feathers and tracking down prey by sound. The heart-shaped, feathered facial disc directs sound into the ears. The ear-openings are of different sizes and placed slightly differently on the head, allowing the owl to obtain an accurate directional fix on a sound. Light-eyed hawk owls such as the Boobook and Barking Owl have less specialised hearing and hunt mainly by sight.

An alert owl constantly bobs its head and may rock from side to side. This is because its huge eyes are fixed in their sockets and cannot swivel to focus. To compensate, an owl can turn its neck 180 degrees to look behind it.

The Barn Owl has a heart-shaped facial disc and large, dark eyes. It may be found anywhere in Australia, sheltering in tree hollows, caves and buildings. It eats mainly mice and rats.

FROGMOUTHS: KOOKABURRAS OF THE NIGHT

When the sun sets, kookaburras sleep and frogmouths take over their role. The two species are much the same size, eat much the same prey and hunt in the same way: they perch; then pounce on likely small creatures. Though the Tawny Frogmouth is sometimes confused with the Boobook Owl, it is not an owl at all. It has a wide, sharp-edged beak surrounded by sensitive bristle-like feathers and small feet that are suited to perching rather than seizing prey. Its call, given at night, is a repeated, far-carrying "oom-oom-oom". During the day, a frogmouth roosts along a branch or in a tree fork, camouflaged by its cryptic coloration. If alarmed, it pokes its beak in the air, heightening its resemblance to the stump of a broken-off branch. A pair builds a stick nest on a branch or in a fork. They take turns to incubate one to three white eggs for around one month, then both feed the young. Family parties of four or five may be seen roosting together.

A Tawny Frogmouth during daytime. The wide beak has sharp edges and is surrounded by touch-sensitive, bristle-like feathers.

At night, a Tawny Frogmouth perches and watches for an insect, frog, mouse or other small creature. It pounces, chomps the prey into submission and swallows it whole.

A TASTE OF HONEY

Australia is home to around 70 species of honeyeaters that range in size from friarbirds of 30 cm long down to tiny spinebills half their size. They are active, often noisy birds plumaged in brown, green or grey, often with white or yellow ear patches. A honeyeater's tongue is long with up-curved sides and a tip divided into four fringed "brushes". When the tip is loaded with nectar, the tongue is squeezed against the roof of the mouth, forcing the sweet liquid down grooves at the tongue's base and into the bird's throat. Honeyeater bills range in length and stoutness; some probe grevilleas and other long, slender flowers, others suit the open blossoms of eucalypts. However, some species bypass the proper entry to a flower by stabbing through the base of the blossom for direct access to the nectar. Most species supplement their nectar diet with insects.

Many honeyeaters have loud, distinctive alarm calls, and let the world know when a hawk, snake or owl is in sight.

The long, slender beak of this Eastern Spinebill can reach deep into a grevillea flower. Only around 15–16 cm long, Eastern and Western Spinebills are amongst the smallest honeyeaters.

A New Holland Honeyeater probes a callistemon flower for nectar. It is one of a group of honeyeaters with yellow flashes on their wings.

BIRDS OF THE ARIDLANDS

LIVING IN A DRY CONTINENT

Much of Australia has low and unpredictable rainfall, but is still home to large numbers of birds. Some of them, such as birds of prey, crows and butcherbirds, may obtain water from their food and need not drink every day. Many, such as doves, pigeons, quails and parrots, need to live near permanent water because their diet of seeds makes it necessary for them to drink regularly. A few, such as the Magpie-lark, martins and swallows, depend on mud as nest-construction material. Nearly all species will drink and bathe readily if water is available.

The aridlands are also home to nomadic species that fly long distances from one area where waterholes and claypans are drying up to others where heavy rains are falling. Sometimes, perhaps navigating by sensitivity to changes in barometric pressure, the newcomers fly in within hours of the downpour beginning. If the rain is heavy enough, desert plants will spring dramatically into leaf, then flower, then set seed. Nomadic birds such as chats and Budgerigars arrive and nest while the bounty lasts, then fly away to find a survival spot until the next inundation. The most dramatic of these nomads are the waterbirds — ducks, ibis, spoonbills, grebes, and, soaring across vast spaces on huge wings, the Black Swan and the Australian Pelican.

Opposite: The Spinifex Pigeon, a seed-eater, needs to drink regularly.

Above: Budgerigars can be found in vast flocks when a good season brings bountiful food.

All parrots are sociable, but the Galah adds a wild, school kid quality to its playfulness. These Galahs are part of a flock gathered at the overflow from a desert artesian bore.

CLOWNS IN THE DESERT

Many people would deny that parrots — or any bird, for that matter — have a sense of humour. Some might even say that no bird "plays" as humans understand the term. However, cockatoos certainly give a good imitation of enjoying not-very-serious social interactions with their own kind. A flock of Galahs may be seen at a billabong or borehole, perching on branches or fence wires, swinging upside down, squawking, ruffling their feathers and sparring with each other. Other cockatoos, especially young ones, also have their times for boisterous behaviour that is often triggered off by events such as a shower of rain after a spell of dry weather or arrival at a windmill where pumped water splashes into a trough.

A pair of Little Corellas in a tall tree beside a desert waterhole, screeching and flapping their wings like a pair of human cheerleaders at a football match.

The Australian Ringneck Parrot has a number of colour forms. This is the mallee form, seen in arid woodland from north-east of the Flinders Ranges, SA, to around Windorah, Qld.

The Black-breasted Buzzard is a tool-using bird of prey. It picks up stones and flings them at the eggs of emus and other ground-nesters. Once the shell is broken, the Buzzard eats the contents.

BIRDS OF PREY

The desert, with its concentrations of birds and other creatures around water, is home to a number of birds of prey. The two shown here are spectacular, whether seen soaring overhead or perched beside some quiet road. Both are opportunistic feeders. The Black-breasted Buzzard is large with long wings, each marked with a prominent white bullseye, and a short tail. It catches reptiles, birds and small mammals, and, if it finds an Emu nest, may break eggs by throwing stones at them with its beak. The Wedge-tailed Eagle is even larger – a female may have a wingspan of over two metres. A young "Wedgie" has a golden head and upper parts; by six years of age it is black. This eagle soars in rising air currents, spotting carrion such as roadkill. It also takes live prey such as rabbits and small kangaroos.

A female Wedge-tailed Eagle may have a wingspan of 2.3 m; the male's reaches 1.85 m.
This young eagle has a golden head and mantle. By six or seven it will be completely black.

One of Australia's animal emblems, the Emu is a large, flightless bird whose double-shafted feathers are soft and filmy. A female may weigh 50 kg and stand nearly 2 m tall.

EMU AND AUSTRALIAN BUSTARD

Large, ground-living birds often prefer wide open spaces. The Emu cannot fly and depends on its long legs to carry it speedily away from potential danger. The Australian Bustard, which takes some time to become airborne, usually freezes, then slowly walks away. This reluctance to take to flight and its large, edible body have left it extremely vulnerable to hunters and foxes, and strict protection has been necessary to restore its numbers somewhat. However, habitat destruction by sheep and rabbits needs to be controlled if the bustard, one of a group becoming rare on the grassy plains of the world, is to be preserved. Both birds eat grass, seeds and small creatures such as mice and grasshoppers. The female bustard incubates one or two spotted eggs on the ground, then cares for the chicks alone. The female Emu courts the male, lays eggs, then leaves him to look after eggs and chicks.

*A male Australian Bustard slowly walks away from a potential threat – the photographer's
vehicle stopped by the side of a desert road.*

A pair of Malleefowl mate for life. Their eggs incubate in a nest in a huge mound of sand.

Each day, the temperature of the mound is adjusted by adding or removing sand.

BIRDS OF THE RAINFORESTS

SINGING IN THE GREEN FORESTS

Australia's rainforests include the tropical forests of the north, the subtropical forests of the central east coast and the temperate forests of Victoria and Tasmania. All forms of rainforest depend on regular, heavy rainfall for survival and are characterised by a closed canopy where the foliage of one tree nearly touches that of its neighbours, blocking most light from the ground below. Rainforest birds make full use of their complex habitat. Some species such as parrots, pigeons, honeyeaters and an array of small insect-eating birds feed in the canopy. Other birds feed and nest on the tree trunks; others live in the vines, epiphytes and lesser trees that form a lower storey; yet others pick over the leaf litter for invertebrates and fruit. These birds include robins, bowerbirds, scrub-wrens, lyrebirds and that vanishing giant of the tropics, the Southern Cassowary.

Rainforest birds are often heard but not seen. The human watcher needs to move quietly, stand still listening and identifying calls, and risk a cricked neck peering up into the canopy, alerted by the patter of fruit on the forest floor to the presence of a parrot, pigeon, or even a riflebird or bowerbird searching for fruits high above.

Above: The Buff-breasted Paradise Kingfisher nests in termite mounds on the rainforest floor.

Opposite: A male Australian King-Parrot amongst new, bronze-coloured forest growth.

The female Eclectus Parrot looks as if she would stand out like a firebrand in the rainforest of North Queensland. However, her gaudy plumage blends into the forest canopy.

CLOAKS OF MANY COLOURS

The feathers that enable a bird to fly and protect it from the weather serve other purposes as well. There are plumage colours typical of each bird species, but within that species colours may differ widely. Male and female may look quite different: the female Eclectus Parrot shown opposite and the male shown below are entirely different colours. Adult and young birds are often different colours, and their feathers may also be different in length (young birds may have longer tail and flight feathers). As the young bird matures, it may moult into yet another plumage before eventually assuming adult colours. A bird's plumage often serves to camouflage the owner in its usual habitat. The Eclectus Parrot may look gaudy, but in the rainforest it melds with foliage and flowers.

A male Eclectus Parrot is mainly green and blue. This one scratches his head with a foot, showing the two-toes-forwards two-toes-backwards formation characteristic of parrots.

The Pied Imperial-Pigeon nests mainly on northern Australia's offshore islands. It eats fruit, including the fruits of several tropical palm trees.

RAINFOREST PIGEONS

Grain-eating pigeons and doves (smaller pigeons) feed in open, grassy places. Their coloration is usually in combinations of sober greys and browns, and, when disturbed, they rocket from the ground at speed, impelled by massive pectoral flight muscles. Rainforest pigeons, in contrast, feed on fruits and berries high in the rainforest canopy or on palm seeds on the forest edges. Some species are coloured in brilliant greens accented with purple, yellow and pink; others are more soberly black and white. They are speedy fliers, capable of roaming long distances in search of fruiting trees. The Pied Imperial-Pigeon nests and roosts on islands off Australia's northern and north-eastern coasts. It feeds on the mainland, and each day flocks may be seen winging their way back and forth over the tropical sea.

Above: The White-headed Pigeon is related to the familiar feral pigeon that flies in city streets. It eats both fruits and seeds.

The male Regent Bowerbird expends his energy in building and maintaining an avenue-style bower, decorating it with fruit and flowers, then displaying there to attract females.

REGENTS RULE, OKAY?

The male Regent Bowerbird, in glistening gold and velvety black plumage, is a spectacular sight as it postures and sings in its bower. Several male and immature Regents may attend one bower, an avenue of twigs built on a loosely constructed platform under vines, ferns or bushes. The bower may be painted yellow with saliva and juice from crushed berries, and be decorated with red-brown leaves, berries, shells and sometimes orange peel. A dominant male whose bower, decorations, songs and postures are better than those of others, will attract most females to mate with him. After mating, the female flies off to build a nest and raise the young on her own.

The female Regent Bowerbird: Females are drabber than males of their species. They choose mates, then go off to build their nests, incubate their eggs and raise their chicks by themselves.

HELMETED HERO OF THE RAINFOREST

Huge, flightless birds lived in the rainforests that covered vast areas of Australia around 35 million years ago. Today, in wet tropical rainforest remnants between Cape York and Townsville, Queensland, there is just one species – the Southern Cassowary.

A cassowary is shorter, stockier and heavier than an Emu, Australia's other flightless land bird. The female cassowary is larger than the male, and has a bigger casque – the large, horny helmet on the head – and bigger feet. She will mate with up to three males in succession in a season, then lays her eggs in a leaf-lined scrape at the nest site. Each male incubates her eggs for around 55 days, then cares for the chicks for a further 9 months.

Cassowaries eat fallen forest fruits and can swallow items up to 6 cm in diameter. Their legs are very powerful, and the sharp nail of the inner toe, used in defence, may be over 12 cm long. Humans do well to avoid being in kicking range. These majestic birds are endangered by habitat loss, as they each need a large area of rainforest in which to feed.

The male Southern Cassowary is smaller than the female, weighing up to 34 kg to her possible 58 kg. He incubates the eggs in a nest on the ground, then rears the striped chicks.

The remarkable helmet, or casque, of the Southern Cassowary probably protects its head when it dashes through rainforest vines and bushes.

Lewin's Honeyeater is one of a group of nectar-eaters that frequents thick vegetation. Its grey-green plumage camouflages it as it searches for flowers and insects.

IN THE FOLIAGE AND ON THE FOREST FLOOR

Rainforest is rich in food and nesting sites. It supports many forms of bird life, each group exploiting a different niche in the habitat.

There are trees flowering somewhere in a forest or on its verges right throughout the year, and honeyeaters take advantage of the bounty. These nectar-eating birds have long tongues with up-curved sides and brushy tips. When the tip is loaded with nectar, the bird pulls it back and squeezes it against the roof of the mouth, forcing nectar down grooves at the tongue's base and into the bird's throat. The plant is paid well for its nectar though; the honeyeater unknowingly transports the fertilising pollen to the next flower visited.

Lyrebirds are creatures of the forest floor, the Superb in south temperate forests, the Albert's further north. A male lyrebird displays with song and dance on a mound he has scratched up in a forest clearing. A female, once she has chosen a male and mated with him, builds a domed nest of sticks, lays one egg, then cares for it – and the chick when it hatches – without any assistance from the male.

The male Superb Lyrebird's tail consists of two outer, barred feathers which frame the "lyre" and enclose 12 filamentous feathers. The tail is raised over the back and quivered in display.

These Eastern Yellow Robin chicks are just out of the nest and enduring the most vulnerable period of their lives.

An Eastern Yellow Robin feeds its chicks. Other, grown-up offspring from a previous nesting may help their parents bring insects to the ever-hungry youngsters.

A male Australian King-Parrot, one of Australia's most spectacular birds.

RULERS IN THEIR OWN FOREST KINGDOM

This brilliantly hued bird was named after Phillip Gidley King, Governor of New South Wales between 1800 and 1806, and was originally called King's Parrot. However, the name gradually became king-parrot, and the bird is indeed monarch of its patch of eastern coastal forest, even to its habit of sitting on a dead branch that rises above the canopy as if surveying its kingdom.

The birds shown here are both males in full plumage. The female has a duller green head and breast, a red belly and yellow eye. An immature king-parrot of either sex has female coloration but brown eyes. A flock will usually contain more birds in female plumage than adult males, and may be an amalgamation of several pairs and their offspring. Although wary and timid in the forest, king-parrots may become very confident on forest verges where human generosity brings them flying in to compete with Crimson Rosellas for handouts of seed. They nest in deep hollows in upright tree trunks.

Adult Australian King-Parrots have yellow eyes. Immatures of either sex have brown eyes.

BIRDS OF THE WETLANDS

WADERS, DIVERS AND AQUABATS

Australia's permanent bodies of fresh water are often isolated or disappearing. Once there were great inland bodies of water that supported thriving human communities as well as the wildlife they hunted. Today, the remaining inland lakes are saline and may remain waterless for years, like Lake Eyre in South Australia, which is 15 m below sea-level, but fills only after substantial rain falls on country far away to the north. When these inland lakes do flood, birds fly in, often from vast distances, to breed before the water evaporates.

Coastal lakes and wetlands are the focus of human settlement. They are being drained, developed and polluted and need to be strictly protected if their birdlife is to survive. The largest aggregations of water birds are to be seen on northern seasonal wetlands that are inundated by annual monsoonal rains.

Australia's waterbirds are both elegant and remarkable. The Comb-crested Jacana (opposite) is one of the most fascinating. It seems to walk on the water, treading across waterlily leaves on impossibly long toes. The male is courted by the female, who lays her eggs in a nest he has constructed then goes off to find other mates. The male hatches out the eggs; he may then carry his chicks under his wings, their fragile legs and long toes dangling down.

Opposite: A Comb-crested Jacana broods its chicks on a tropical swamp.

Above: A Plumed Whistling-Duck shakes water from its tail after diving.

PREDATORS OF COASTS AND ESTUARIES

The Osprey, the Brahminy Kite and the White-bellied Sea-Eagle all catch fish and all have unfeathered legs. While the sea-eagle snatches its prey from the surface and does not get its plumage wet, the Osprey may plunge into the water, or even be dragged beneath the surface until it manages to lift its prey with strong beats of its long, kinked wings. The soles of an Osprey's feet are spiky, and it holds its fish with one foot on either side so that the sometimes awkwardly shaped prey is carried head-first.

The Brahminy Kite also takes live prey. One adult of a pair nesting in tall mangroves was even observed bringing a large, still-wriggling seasnake to its half-grown chick.

The Brahminy Kite may be seen on the estuaries of larger rivers in northern Australia. It builds its stick nest high in a tree. The juvenile plumage is streaked brown and fawn.

The Osprey has become rare in many parts of the Northern Hemisphere but is still often seen around Australia's coasts and lakes. It is more common in the north of the continent.

A female White-bellied Sea-Eagle measures up to 84 cm from beak to tail-tip. Perched, the wings are longer than the tail. The sea-eagle's call is a loud, goose-like "ang-ank".

LORD OF THE WATERS

The White-bellied Sea-Eagle can be seen around Australia's coastline and on large inland rivers and lakes. On some northern coastal rivers where prey is common, the enormous stick nests of these majestic birds decorate tall trees at regular intervals. On coasts and islands, if trees of suitable size are lacking, sea-eagles will build on headlands or on the ground. The white, fluffy chick moults into a juvenile plumage of speckled slaty brown, with a large white bullseye in each wing. This is eventually exchanged for the adult's striking grey and white. Sea-eagles are dashing hunters, soaring high, then dropping to better viewing height when they first spot prey. Fish are seized after a spectacular feet-first dive, which ends with the victim being plucked from the water by huge talons. Freshwater turtles and waterbirds as large as Brolgas and Magpie Geese are also on the menu. Sea-eagles will also feed on carrion, which makes an easy meal.

In flight, an adult White-bellied Sea-Eagle displays its white underparts and dramatically marked wings and tail. Soaring, it looks like an immense, pied butterfly.

While one Yellow-billed Spoonbill broods small chicks, its partner stands by.

WITH A SILVER SPOON

Spoonbills have delightful family lives. A pair builds a stick nest in a tree beside or in water. The two to four eggs are brooded conscientiously, then the chicks are fed small water creatures by their parents. Spoonbill parents preen each other and their nestlings. There is little of the sibling rivalry often seen in herons and egrets: as the chicks grow older, they emulate their parents, preening each other and their parents' heads and necks as well.

These large waterbirds fly with their necks and bills extended. They hunt by wading through shallow water, swishing their bills from side to side, snapping up water creatures in reflexes that take only 0.01 of a second between touch and grab. The Yellow-billed Spoonbill can be seen on swamps, lakes and billabongs and may also spend time on farm dams. In the breeding season, it grows stiff nuptial plumes on its breast and from the back of its head.

A spoonbill latecomer flies to roost with others on a dead tree standing in a swamp.

A Comb-crested Jacana takes off from a lilypad. It lives in wetlands of northern Australia, from the Kimberley in the west to Cape York in the east, and halfway down the east coast.

DAGGER-BILLED GEMS

Australia's kingfishers all have long, dagger-like bills and weak feet. Some belong to a group known as the forest kingfishers, which have a black band through the eye and a stouter bill. They may be seen far from water as they feed on insects, lizards and other small terrestrial prey, and nest in burrows drilled into earthen banks or arboreal termite mounds. The two fishing kingfishers, the Azure and the Little, catch their prey in water and have long, slender beaks and short tails. Their white eggs are laid in tunnel nests dug into earth banks. Australia's two kookaburra species are also kingfishers, the giants of their kind.

The Forest Kingfisher may take fish or tadpoles if they are easily caught, but is equally satisfied with grasshoppers, cicadas and other insects, frogs and small lizards.

The Azure Kingfisher is one of two Australian kingfisher species that finds its food in water.

It perches above a creek or other water source, waiting to dive in and catch a fish or yabby.

THERE'S SAFETY IN NUMBERS

Australia's waterfowl often lay numerous eggs, but may raise only a few ducklings, goslings or cygnets to independence. Unpredictable water conditions, and predators from the land (including introduced species such as foxes and cats), the water (turtles, fish and snakes) and the air (harriers, kites and swamphens) account for many fluffy youngsters. The young of the Australian Shelduck shown below are guarded by their parents (the female, with the white-ringed eye, is at left).

The duck, swan or goose that survives to maturity has discovered that there is safety in numbers. Out of the breeding season, mature waterfowl protect themselves by flocking. A predator may be confused by the sheer numbers of possible victims and a few sentinels can keep watch while the rest of the flock feeds.

A pair of Australian Shelducks and their well-grown brood rest on an island in a lake.
The parents are ever-watchful for danger.

Large flocks of waterbirds gather where food is abundant. This is part of a gathering of Plumed Whistling Ducks on the wetlands of Kakadu National Park, Northern Territory.

A male Darter displays the wide gape that allows it to swallow big fish. Each fish is speared underwater, carried to the surface, flicked off the beak and swallowed.

WATERBIRDS OF NIGHT AND DAY

The Darter must be one of Australia's most noticeable waterbirds even though it does not occur in great numbers and hunts its fishy prey under water. However, after leaving the water, it picks a sunny perch, spreads its wings wide and suns itself at length. It is made conspicuous by its size (about 90 cm from bill-tip to tail-tip), dramatic pied coloration and elegant, snaky neck. Theories vary about why Darters and cormorants bask. One is that they are drying their feathers. Another is that by sunning and muscle-quivering they are warming themselves after swallowing cold fish.

Humans seldom see the Nankeen Night-Heron because it hunts after dark. Camouflaged by its sombre plumage, it spends its day roosting in thick foliage. At sunset, its flies quietly off to hunt for fish, frogs, yabbies and tadpoles.

A Nankeen Night-Heron settles onto its fishing perch at dusk after sleeping through the day. Its white plumes signal that the owner is in breeding condition.

BEAUTIES OF THE BILLABONGS

Herons and egrets are members of the same family group of birds. With their long legs, long necks and slender bills, these elegant birds are ideally suited to taking their prey in shallow water and wet grasslands. The stocky, relatively short-necked Cattle Egret usually feeds on dry land, snapping up insects disturbed by grazing stock. However, like other group members, it roosts and nests over water.

In the breeding season, egrets and herons grow sprays of filmy plumes on their breasts, backs and heads. In the nineteenth century, nesting egrets were slaughtered for these aigrettes, which were used to decorate hats and make fans. The plume trade was outlawed in Australia after H.H. Mattingley's photographs revealed to the public that egret chicks starved to death because their parents had been killed for human adornment.

A Great Egret stands like a porcelain figurine, watching for an unwary fish or yabby.

The exquisite Pied Heron lives in northern wetlands.

Australian Pelicans often hunt by forming a circle then scooping up fish. The bird on the right demonstrates how the huge bill can be used with precision to preen the plumage.

The three forward-directed toes of a Magpie Goose have half-webs between them. These large waterfowl wade through shallow water, grazing on aquatic vegetation.

IT TAKES THREE TO RAISE BABIES

The reedy northern wetlands in which Magpie Geese breed are the haunt of many predators, ranging from crocodiles, file snakes and water pythons to long-necked turtles, barramundi and sea-eagles. A pair of geese finds it difficult to raise their brood without losing some or all of the goslings to these menaces. Many Magpie Geese form trios of two females and one male: observations show that such trios have far better chances of bringing their goslings to maturity than do pairs. The nest is a large mound of vegetation built amongst emerging rushes or grasses. Flocks gather to breed when the summer monsoon rains fill wetlands. As the season proceeds, they may fly off in huge flocks to graze where new growth is available. In the past, this has led to some conflict between the interests of the Magpie Geese and those of aspiring rice-farmers.

A flock of Magpie Geese takes to the air from a Northern Territory wetland.

BIRDS OF THE COASTS

A NEVER-ENDING COASTLINE OF BIRDS

Australia is an enormous island with a vastly variable coastline. At the extremes are the mangrove swamps and mudflats of the north and the sheer limestone cliffs that fall into the Great Australian Bight in the south. In between are rocky headlands and sandy beaches, wave-cut offshore platforms and continental islands, river estuaries and coastal lagoons. Each type of coast has its resident birds, supplemented in spring and autumn by migrants travelling to and from their northern hemisphere breeding grounds.

Some coastal birds make their living probing sand or mud exposed by low tide. Others catch crabs, molluscs and mudskippers on mangrove mudflats. A few fish in shallows and pools. However, the most exciting are the long-winged aerobats that plunge or swoop into the sea to grab, gulp or spear surface-swimming fish. Terns and noddies, boobies and gannets, albatrosses, shearwaters, gulls and skuas – all depend on the bounty of the oceans. Frigatebirds have an additional trick. Superb fliers, they add to their self-caught menu the fish carried by other seabirds, harassing their victims mercilessly until they disgorge their hard-won prizes, then scooping the booty up before it hits the water.

Opposite: The Black-naped Tern nests on islands off northern and north-eastern Australia.

Above: Pied Oystercatchers pry open bivalve mollusc shells to get at the creatures within.

Coral cays provide many seabirds with roosting and nesting refuges. This flock of Crested Terns will go fishing when tide and wind are right.

BIRD OF THE TROPIC SEAS

Tropicbirds, as William Dampier remarked in the late 1600s, are creatures seldom seen outside tropical waters. However, the Red-tailed Tropicbird may nest as far south as Sugarloaf Rock in the south-west of Western Australia. The tropicbird is one of the most beautiful of seabirds, a superb flier distinguished by two long central tail feathers, red in one Australian species, white in the other. These feathers inspired seamen of the sailing days to bestow on the bird the nickname Bosun-bird, for the bosun (boatswain) of a sailing ship carried a long, thin metal spike for unravelling strands of rope. Tropicbirds nest under rock overhangs, usually on offshore islands or coral cays. Attempts to nest on the mainland are comparatively unsuccessful.

The Red-tailed Tropicbird is a superb flier. This one has moulted one long tail feather.

A Red-tailed Tropicbird with its dark-eyed, downy chick.

The Pacific Gull (above) is being challenged by the Kelp Gull, which came from New Zealand in 1943. The Kelp lacks the black tail band and has red on the bottom mandible only.

SEAFRONT SCAVENGERS

Think back to youthful adventures on any southern Australian beach, and the memory always features the cries of the Silver Gull. This omnivorous bird swoops above or stands around picnickers, eying them with greedy silver eyes, waiting for edibles, whether offered or simply left unguarded. Where human handouts are not available, Silver Gulls eat flotsam and the eggs and small chicks of other seabirds. They are not above hanging around rubbish dumps, playing fields and the streets of seaside towns, and may be seen on inland waters as well as around the coastline.

The Pacific Gull is half as big again as the Silver Gull. It is a bird of southern shorelines that feeds on marine creatures and debris. A Pacific Gull may fly aloft with a mollusc, then drop it onto rocks to crack the shell open and expose the tasty animal within.

The Silver Gull is one of Australia's commonest seabirds. It prefers to nest on islands, often near colonies of other seabirds, where it can steal eggs and chicks to eat.

*Smallest of its flightless group, the Little Penguin nests in burrows on Australia's southern
beaches. When the chicks hatch, the adults return from the sea each night to feed them.*

A Masked Booby and young chick. The nostrils of boobies are covered with bone. Air is breathed in under the flexible, flared edges of the upper mandible.

DIVING FOR DINNER

Gannets and boobies are closely related, but gannets live in temperate seas while boobies are found in the tropics. Old-time seamen probably named the latter "boobies" from the Spanish word bobo, meaning fool, because they were so easy to approach and kill while nesting. Both gannets and boobies have slender, cigar-shaped bodies, long, pointed wings and wedge-shaped tails. They are very manoeuvrable in the air, and can quickly half-fold their wings and plunge-dive to take fish. Just as the bird's beak pierces the water, the wings are folded back along the body to streamline it. Air-sacs under the skin of breast and abdomen cushion the shock of hitting the water; the nostrils are closed off by bone, and air is sucked in under the flared edges of the upper beak.

An adult Masked Booby feeding its chick. The chick takes the food from its parent's gullet.

An Eastern Reef Egret contemplates its chances of catching a final fish before sunset.

BIRDS ON A CORAL CAY

A coral cay, a tropical island formed by coral debris, is a splendid place to enjoy the beauty of seabirds and to watch them at close quarters. Eastern Reef Egrets perch on exposed lumps of coral, stabbing at unwary fish passing below. Their nests are in casuarina trees or pandanus palms. Terns and noddies stand dozing on the sand or perch on coral rubble waiting for the right moment to fly out to sea.

Terns nest above high-tide mark or amongst coral rubble while darker-plumaged noddies build their nests amongst pisonia foliage. When the nest-trees bear their sticky seeds, noddies, and the shearwaters that nest in ground burrows in the pisonia groves, are in danger of becoming so entangled in the adhesive bundles that they can no longer fly.

A noddy preens its plumage before flying out to sea searching for small surface fish.

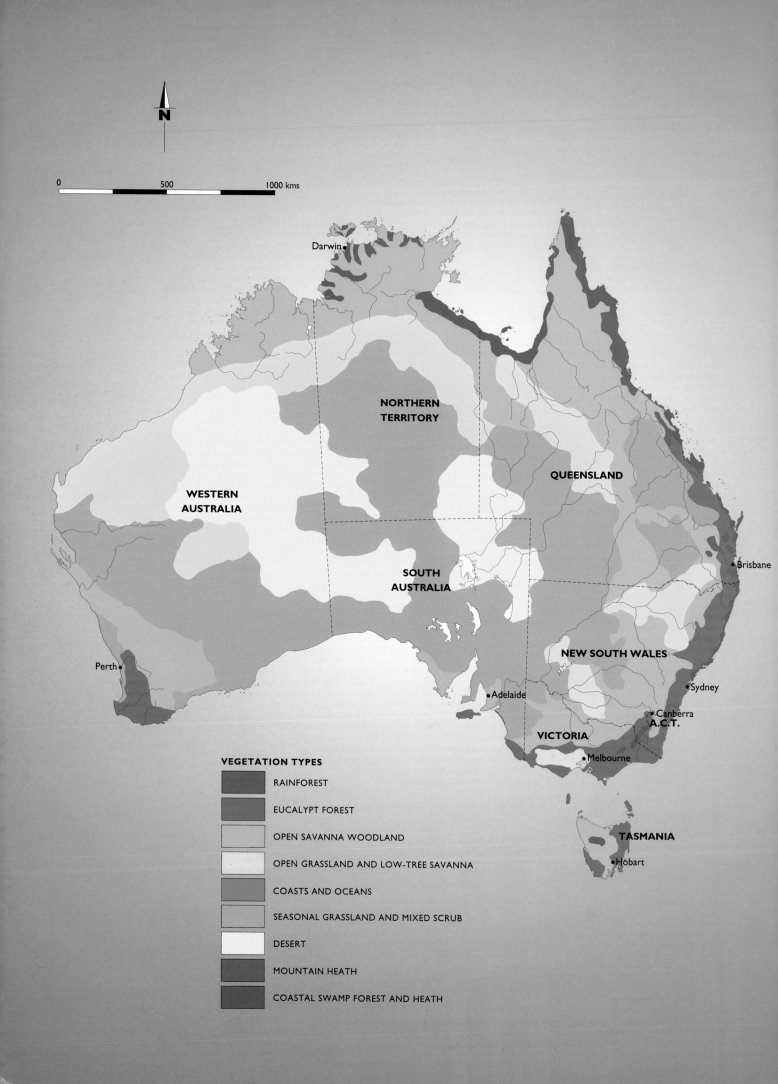

N

0   500   1000 kms

DARWIN•

NORTHERN
TERRITORY

WESTERN
AUSTRALIA

Perth•

QUEENSLAND

SOUTH
AUSTRALIA

Brisbane•

NEW SOUTH WALES

•Sydney

•Adelaide

•Canberra
A.C.T.

VICTORIA

•Melbourne

TASMANIA

•Hobart

VEGETATION TYPES

RAINFOREST

EUCALYPT FOREST

OPEN SAVANNA WOODLAND

OPEN GRASSLAND AND LOW-TREE SAVANNA

COASTS AND OCEANS

SEASONAL GRASSLAND AND MIXED SCRUB

DESERT

MOUNTAIN HEATH

COASTAL SWAMP FOREST AND HEATH

WHY WATCH BIRDS?

There are many reasons why looking at birds and watching their behaviour are such popular occupations. Some people simply enjoy travelling and seeing birds in exotic settings while others prefer to watch the feathered creatures that come to their backyard feeders. Many revel in compiling daily and lifetime lists of the birds they have seen. The behaviour of birds fascinates observers, and their sheer beauty and mastery of the air inspire artists and photographers, composers and poets. A good pair of binoculars and as many bird books as you can afford are useful aids to birdwatching. Membership of a birdwatcher's club or some other group of bird enthusiasts will bring you into contact with like-minded souls with whom you can adventure, compare notes and relive triumphs of twitching (racing to places where rare or unusual species have been spotted).

A pair of White-breasted Woodswallows. One is preening. The other is mantling — relaxing by stretching one wing and one leg.

INDEX

Bee-eater, Rainbow 23

Black-Cockatoo, Glossy 16

 Yellow-tailed 16

Booby, Masked 90, 91

Bowerbird, Great 20, 21

 Regent 48, 49

Budgerigar 31

Bustard, Australian 39

Buzzard, Black-breasted 36, 37

Cassowary, Southern 50, 51

chats 30

Cockatoo

 (see also Black-Cockatoo)

 Galah 16, 32, 33

 Gang-Gang 16

 Sulphur-crested 16, 17

Corella, Little 33

 Slender-billed 16

Darter 72, 73

Duck, Plumed Whistling 59, 71

Eagle, Wedge-tailed 37

egrets 7, 74

 Cattle 74

 Eastern Reef 92, 93

 Great 74

Emu 38, 39

fairy-wrens 22

Finch, Long-tailed 18

 Red-browed 19

friarbirds 28

frigatebirds 81

Frogmouth, Tawny 26, 27

Galah 16, 32, 33

gannets 91

Goose, Magpie 78, 79

Gull, Kelp 86

 Pacific 86

 Silver 87

herons 7, 74

 Pied 75

 Nankeen Night- 73

Honeyeater, Lewin's 52

 New Holland 28

Imperial-Pigeon, Pied 46, 47

Jabiru (see Black-necked Stork)

Jacana, Comb-crested 58, 59, 66–67

King-Parrot, Australian 42, 56, 57

Kingfisher (see also Kookaburra)

 Azure 68

 Buff-breasted Paradise 43

 Forest 68

 Little 68

Kite, Brahminy 60

Kookaburra, Laughing 4, 7, 68

Lorikeet, Purple-crowned 8

 Rainbow 1, 10, 11

Lyrebird, Albert's 53

 Superb 53

magpies 7

Malleefowl 40–41

noddies 93

Osprey 60, 61

Owl, Barking 24, 25

 Barn 25

 Boobook 25, 26

Oystercatcher, Pied 81

Parrot, Australian King- 42, 56, 57

 Australian Ringneck 34–35

 Eclectus 44, 45

Pelican, Australian 76–77

Penguin, Little 88–89

Pigeon, Pied Imperial- 46, 47

 Spinifex 30

 White-headed 47

Robin, Eastern Yellow 54–55

 Scarlet 9

Rosella, Crimson 2–3, 14, 15, 57

 Eastern 12–13, 15

Sea-Eagle, White-bellied 60, 62, 63

shearwaters 93

Shelduck, Australian 70

spinebills 28

 Eastern 29

 Western 29

Spoonbill, Yellow-billed 64, 65

Stork, Black-necked 6

terns 7, 93

 Black-naped 80

 Crested 82–83

Tropicbird, Red-tailed 84, 85

Woodswallows, White-breasted 95